"Mouw offers advice that is not only informative but also encouraging to evangelical scholars and those considering a scholarly vocation. Herein are sage virtues needed for the evangelical scholarly pursuit."

— AMOS YONG
Fuller Seminary

"A refreshing reminder that cultivating our thought life and scholarship can only be done when we also keep in touch with the Lord. These musings from an experienced Christian leader will be solid food for Christian scholars everywhere."

— DARRELL BOCK
Dallas Theological Seminary

"Mouw assures us that we can navigate the perilous terrain of the hyper-critical, the fragmentation of knowledge, the isolation, all the while attending to the One in whom all reality coheres. I can hear him saying, 'You can do this.' "

— CHERYL BRIDGES JOHNS
Princeton Theological Seminary

"Winsome guidance. . . . Every evangelical scholar will benefit from reading these essays based on a life of leadership in the evangelical academy."

— ROGER E. OLSON
Truett Seminary, Baylor University

Called to the Life of the Mind

Some Advice for Evangelical Scholars

RICHARD J. MOUW

WILLIAM B. EERDMANS PUBLISHING COMPANY
Grand Rapids, Michigan / Cambridge, U.K.

Published 2014 by
WM. B. EERDMANS PUBLISHING CO.
2140 Oak Industrial Drive N.E., Grand Rapids, Michigan 49505 /
P.O. Box 163, Cambridge CB3 9PU U.K.

Printed in the United States of America

20 19 18 17 16 15 14   7 6 5 4 3 2 1

Library of Congress Cataloging-in-Publication Data

Mouw, Richard J.
Called to the life of the mind:
some advice for evangelical scholars / Richard J. Mouw.
    pages   cm
ISBN 978-0-8028-6766-7 (pbk.: alk. paper)
1. Theology — Study and teaching — United States.
2. Evangelicalism — United States.   3. Mouw, Richard J.
4. Theologians.   I. Title.

BV4030.M68   2014
230′.046240973 — dc23

2014033463

www.eerdmans.com

Contents

CONTENTS

ONE

The Price

I WASN'T SUPPOSED TO spend my life in the world of scholarship. At least that was not what my family had in mind. I was an evangelical preacher's son, and the pressure to follow in my father's footsteps was strong. In my early spiritual environs, higher education was something you suffered through in order to be able to get on with the Lord's real work: the urgent business of proclaiming the Gospel in all of its simplicity and power.

This "simple-Gospel" emphasis was reinforced by considerable anti-intellectual rhetoric from the pulpits. I remember clearly the loud "amens" that one traveling revival preacher evoked when he told us that, in contrast to what he had learned in the few seminary courses he had taken, "you don't need exegesis, you just need Jesus!" All that the worldly intellectuals have to offer, another pulpiteer warned us, is a bunch of "fool-osophies." And there was much more: "Education is a good thing only if you get the victory over it." "The only school any Christian needs to attend is the Holy Ghost's school of the Bible." And so on.

As a student at a large public high school in New Jersey, I belonged to a teenage Bible club composed of students at that school who got together regularly to encourage each other in our Christian walk. One day an alumna of our little group came back to visit us. She had graduated from our high school the year before and was now a student at a large public university. She was home on her spring break and she visited our group to tell us what it was like to be a Christian on a secular university campus. I will never forget her testimony. She told us about a philosophy course she had been taking. It was a very weird subject, she said. The professor tried to get them to ask questions like, What is truth? What is goodness? What is reality? At one point in the course, she reported, he even asked them to think about whether the desks in their rooms continued to exist when no one was perceiving them.

We agreed with her: that was pretty weird stuff. Indeed we shook our heads in disbelief that sensible people could waste their time with such strange thoughts. And then she said something that made a deep impression on me. "I'm glad that I am a Christian," she said, "because that means that I don't have to worry about such things. When you know that Christ is the answer, then you don't have to worry about the questions!"

I remember my reaction well. I was inspired by her straightforward and unadorned faith. And I silently prayed that I too would always have the kind of simple confidence that would keep me from being carried away by philosophical speculation.

But, alas, it was not to be. By the time I got to my sophomore year of college, I realized I was in big trouble. I was actually enjoying my liberal arts education — including philosophy courses in which we asked whether the desks in our rooms continued to exist when we did not perceive them! I had even started thinking that maybe I wanted to spend the rest of my life studying and teaching that kind of thing.

Here I was, then, a student at Christian liberal arts college who was finding my studies an exciting intellectual adventure. What was happening to me? I worried much that not only was I disappointing my family's hopes for me, but I was also rebelling against the plans that the Lord himself had for my life.

Then one day a guest speaker came to speak in our chapel. Frank Gaebelein, the son of the editor of the Scofield Bible, was a well-known evangelical leader in his own right. He wrote learned articles in Christian magazines and was the headmaster of the Stony Brook School, a prestigious Christian prep school on Long Island.

In contrast to the secularist outlook, said Gaebelein, Christians must insist that "our intellectual life is infused with faith." But that does not mean that Christian intellectual activity is an easy thing. We must pay a price if we are to use our minds to glorify God. "And the price will not come down. It is nothing less than the discipline of self-restraint and plain hard work."

I can quote Gaebelein accurately because his talk that day, titled "The Christian's Intellectual Life," was later published in a book of his collected writings.[1] But even if I did not have the exact words before me, I would not, more than five decades later, have forgotten the thrust of what he had to say. Hearing him was special experience — I see it as a gift from God — that set me on the course of a lifelong commitment to Christian scholarship.

TWO

Accusing Voices

MAKING A COMMITMENT TO the life of the mind, though, did not end my struggle with anti-intellectualism.

On an autumn day in 1970, I traveled from my Michigan home to the Philosophy Department at the University of Chicago for the final oral defense of my Ph. D. dissertation. I gave myself plenty of time, and I arrived at the university with several hours to spare.

Wandering around the campus, I realized that I was quite apprehensive, even though I had no real worries about navigating this final exercise in my graduate program. As I sat in a campus coffee shop, reflecting on my mood, I realized that my inner turmoil had to do with a feeling of guilt in response to some accusing voices inside of me. They were Christian voices from my past, and they spoke the familiar language of that long line of preachers, Bible teachers, and family members. You have compromised with the world, this voice said. You have followed ways of thinking that are not fitting for a child of God.

When you clear this final hurdle, it is Satan who will claim the real victory.

I did my best to silence those voices for the next few hours, but later that day, making the long drive back home to Grand Rapids after my successful dissertation defense, I argued back. I told the voices that their accusations were misguided. I was deeply grateful for my years of graduate study and for what I saw — and still see — as a genuine divine call to pursue a career of intellectual exploration, scholarship, and teaching.

Still, I also thanked the voices. And this is important for me to report now. I was grateful to those voices for making me aware of the dangers associated with the intellectual life. You overstate your case, I told the voices, but you are not completely wrong in your basic concerns.

I find it important to continue to stay in dialogue with those voices. They express the concerns of classic Christian pietism — which has often viewed the intellectual life against the background of a cosmic spiritual battle in which the human intellect, especially as it aligns itself with the cause of the academy, is inevitably on the wrong side of the struggle.

And in that continuing dialogue I find it necessary to concede two important points to the accusing voices. One is that there is indeed a spiritual struggle going on in the cosmos. The other is that the intellect does indeed often promote the wrong side of this struggle.

This means that as a Christian I need to be careful not simply to argue for the life of the mind as such — or for the intrinsic value of teaching and scholarship, which are the typical preoccupations of those committed to the life of the mind. Rather, I have an obligation to think carefully about the faithful cultivation of the life of the mind and its primary preoccupations.

I have found it helpful to listen carefully to some Christians' expressions of anti-intellectualism. Here, for example, is a comment from the opening page of the great devotional classic *The Imitation of Christ,* where Thomas à Kempis urges us to forsake the pseudo-wisdom of "the world" in order to render our lives wholly "conformable to Christ":

> What use is it to you to argue loftily about the Trinity, if by your lack of humility you are displeasing to the Trinity? For lofty words make no man holy or just; but a life of virtue endears a man to God. My choice is rather to be pricked to the heart for sin than to have the skill to define the word compunction. If you knew the whole Bible scientifically, and the words of the Philosophers; what good would it all be, that loveless and graceless knowledge? Vanity of vanities and all is vanity except to love God and serve him alone. This is the sum of wisdom; despising the world, to make for the kingdom of heaven.[2]

As stated, this exhortation presents us with false choices. Kempis is certainly right to insist that it is regrettable when a person can set forth all sorts of arguments defending the Trinity but, for all of that, is living a life that displeases the Trinity. He is also correct in his observation that it is better actually to experience compunction than to be able to define the word "compunction" when you have never experienced it in your soul. And, yes, graceless knowledge is surely something to be avoided.

But there is obviously another way to construe all of this. We can insist that it is a good thing for some people both to be able to speak carefully about Trinitarian dogma and to live lives that are pleasing to the Triune God. And that there is something to be said for combining a grasp of the meaning of the word "compunction" with a genuine experience of what this word defines. And surely one alternative to pursuing a graceless knowing is the cultivation of graceful knowledge.

THREE

The Value Question

THERE IS MORE TO the Kingdom of God than academic pursuit. That is an obvious thing to say. God certainly wants us to acknowledge the gifts of people who function outside of the academy — even to absorb their wisdom.

At a gathering of seminary faculty members representing a broad spectrum of church traditions, we were discussing the purposes of theological education. The formulation we were focusing on was the idea that theological education should aim at "the knowledge of God." In a lengthy discussion of what it means to "know God," one person proposed that to know God properly requires that we have a fairly technical grasp of various concepts related to God's nature. This proposal seemed to go over well with most of the other participants, but it made me uneasy.

I was disturbed and so I asked the group: Doesn't this make the knowledge of God primarily an intellectual exercise? After all, if knowing God properly requires that we grasp certain concepts about God's nature, then we would have to conclude that those people who haven't thought a lot about those concepts really don't know God as truly as those who have done a lot of thinking about those concepts.

"Well," a colleague responded, "what would be wrong with saying that?" I replied that I found his suggestion to be very elitist. And then I added what I thought was an impressive rhetorical touch: "Surely you don't think that Mother Teresa would have understood God better had she gone to seminary!" Much to my surprise, my colleague confessed that he did think that Mother Teresa would have known God better if she had received a seminary education.

I think that this perspective is seriously misguided. Not everyone is called to cultivate the life of the mind in a disciplined manner. Some servants of the Lord are fitted for different things. Certainly that was true of Mother Teresa. Our job as intellectuals is not to disdain her calling, but to respect her gifts — and perhaps even to study her — in the way that, say, musical theorists might study a prodigy who plays the violin marvelously with almost no formal training in the art.

Not everyone in the Christian community needs to be seriously involved in intellectual pursuits. But it is important — crucially so — that the Christian community have some people who are cultivating the intellectual disciplines. While I do not regret, even in the smallest degree, that Mother Teresa was not well educated, I am glad that she could serve, and draw strength from, a larger Christian community that supports the intellectual enterprise.

Engaging in serious scholarship is not a prerequisite for an individual's serving the Lord effectively, but the overall patterns of effective Christian service will not be very healthy unless there is communal support from and for good teachers and scholars.

When I was teaching in the Philosophy Department at Calvin College, one of my older colleagues liked to tell a story about a conversation he had once overheard between two undergraduate women. The two students were talking in the hallway outside his office. His door was slightly ajar, so he could hear what they were saying — especially since the conversation was impassioned. The boyfriend of one of the young women had just broken up with her, and she was distraught, sobbing loudly. Her friend tried to comfort her, but none of her therapeutic strategies seemed to be working. Finally, the would-be counselor made a bold pastoral move. "Look," she said, "you've just got to be philosophical about this!" "What do you mean?" the distraught young woman asked through her tears. To which her friend replied: "Just don't think about it!"

This is a story I have told often, not only to philosophy students the first day of a course, but also when praising the scholarly life in general. Whatever pastoral value that piece of advice may have had to the grieving college student, it is not a good understanding of philosophy or any other academic pursuit. A healthy Christian community is one in which at least a segment of that community is encouraged, on behalf of the whole, to "think about it" in consistent and rigorous ways.

FOUR

The Need for Calisthenics

IT IS LATE AUGUST. Driving by the local high school athletic field, I see the football team practicing. Their opening game is weeks away. As I pass, all of the team members are on the ground doing push-ups.

Arriving at Fuller's campus a few minutes later, I have a conversation with a seminary student. He has been spending a part of his summer studying Hebrew. He is frustrated, he tells me. "I feel called to be a pastor," he says, "and I can't see any connection between memorizing Hebrew vocabulary and what I will be doing in ministry. I know I will never use that stuff!"

I talk to him about the high school football team I just saw. I doubt that the team's star quarterback, I say, asks about the connection between doing calisthenics on a lazy late summer afternoon and throwing a completed pass to the cheers of the fans in the bleachers on a Friday night in October. It is not unlike, I tell the seminarian, the connection between memorizing Hebrew vocabulary now and someday addressing the hopes and fears of a congregation gathered for worship.

Philosopher and spiritual writer Simone Weil comments on that kind of connection in her wonderful essay "Reflections on the Right Use of School Studies with a View to the Love of God." Suppose, she says, a person spends an hour trying to find a solution to a difficult geometry problem, without any success. That time is not wasted, she insists, because in some mysterious way important progress has been made. In a subtle way, says Weil, "this apparently barren effort has brought more light into the soul." And the progress for the life of the mind may in fact have nothing to do with mathematics as such. It might turn out that "he who made the unsuccessful effort will one day be able to grasp the beauty of a line of Racine more vividly on account of it."[3]

FIVE

Not Too Much Haste

A PERSON I GREATLY admire for his piety once ad-
dressed our Fuller Seminary faculty on the need for
a committed prayer life. "If every person at this seminary
would spend just ten minutes a day in serious prayer," he
said, "think of the spiritual power that would be unleashed
on this campus!"

On a later occasion I had the opportunity to lead the
same faculty in a devotional meditation. I began by endors-
ing that person's call to a committed prayer life. But then
I added another word of exhortation. "If every person at
this seminary would spend just ten minutes a day simply
thinking clearly, imagine the intellectual power that would
be unleashed on this campus!"

If that smacks of the notion that intellectual activity has
"intrinsic" value, so be it. Disciplined thinking certainly
has pragmatic value — it can serve as the "calisthenics"
that equip us for highly visible things that people can cheer
about. But sustained and disciplined intellectual activity
also has value apart from its pragmatic results.

John Henry Newman had it right in his classic *The Idea of a University.* He was deeply disturbed by those in his day who opposed any notion of "disinterested" learning, who insisted that higher education should aim directly at cultivating those skills necessary for professional engagement.

Newman countered this professionalizing tendency by arguing against "the fallacy . . . that no education is useful that does not teach some temporal calling, or some mechanical art, or some physical secret."[4] A "cultivated intellect," he insisted, is "a good in itself." But he did not, on the other hand, deny a "useful" dimension to disciplined intellectual pursuits. A rigorous liberal education does promote the general goals of the professions in that the "training of the intellect, which is best for the individual himself, best enables him to discharge his duties to society. . . . It prepares him to fill any post with credit, and to master any subject with facility."[5]

Newman's point is an important one. We need to think of the long-term benefits of a clear and disciplined intellectual life. But that does not rule out a concern for visible short-term benefits. I see no reason why higher education cannot also look to practical consequences in the professions — I would not be in a theological seminary if I denied the demonstrable usefulness of serious scholarship for practical areas of service.

What evangelicals have to keep in mind, though, is the danger of allowing a concern for the practical value of learning to merge with lingering tendencies toward anti-intellectualism in the evangelical movement. There is a tendency to see the work of the Kingdom as so urgent that we must move ahead, even without proper intellectual preparation. "O Zion, haste, thy mission high fulfilling." In the 1880s, F. W. Farr, of the Nyack Missionary Training Institute, expressed the "haste" mentality succinctly: "It is best to know and to do," he affirmed, "but it is better to do without knowing than to know without doing."[6]

My own sense is that while we should certainly hope for an ultimate integration of knowing and doing, we ought not to be too worried that our knowing will somehow go to waste if we do not connect it to an immediate doing. What we must ask is whether God can use the kind of knowing that Newman sees as a "good in itself" for the furtherance of the goals of Christ's Kingdom, even when only God knows how that furtherance will actually be expedited.

It is one thing to say, then, that Christian scholarship must aim at promoting the goals of Christ's Kingdom, and another to say that, in order to qualify as genuinely "Christian," the scholarship must aim directly at fulfilling some religiously important goal.

A theologian was addressing a group of Christian scholars. He insisted that Christian scholarship, in order to be worthy of the label, must always be directly linked to "liberating the oppressed." Sitting near me in the audience was a young woman just starting on her career as a chemistry professor. I wondered: suppose she is at a point where she has to choose between moving toward a "pure" area of theoretical research, such as chemical kinetics, or taking on a research project that has clear implications for improving the lot of HIV-AIDS orphans in Africa. Was the theologian at the podium giving her a clear criterion for deciding?

I think not. If "liberating the oppressed" is going to function as our overarching rubric for scholarship, we need to be sure we are operating with a fairly broad sense of "oppression." People are oppressed by many things. We do the economically deprived and the politically persecuted no favors if we act as if they do not need access to knowledge and beauty. A Christian understanding of human flourishing has to cherish a world in which there is good poetry, proper historical understanding, and the benefits of scientific research.

If, then, our young scientist is especially gifted in theoretical chemistry, she might do well to work diligently in that field. We ought to want a world in which that kind of knowledge is valued. It is a good thing simply to cultivate insights into the deep patterns of God's creation — and doing it as people who have been called to love what God has created.

SIX

The Disillusionment

IN OUR ATTITUDES TOWARD what is going on in the world around us, we evangelicals often present ourselves with a false choice. Either we try to separate ourselves as much as possible from the larger culture, or we think we have to attempt to dominate it. Withdrawal — or takeover. We seem to have a hard time reckoning with the thought that God might be calling us to do a third thing: doing the best we can to be an influence for the good without actually gaining any sort of cultural control. We need to find the kind of cultural engagement Mennonite theologian John Howard Yoder taught me to appreciate. We need, he said, to engage culture "in the time of God's patience."

This "false-choice" dichotomy — withdrawal or take-over — often plagues our evangelical attitudes towards scholarship. In the United States the withdrawal mentality held sway for, roughly, the first half of the twentieth century. When the fundamentalists battled against the emerging Protestant liberalism at the beginning of that century, the struggle was for — among other things — control of the theological schools. When the fundamentalists lost the battle within the mainline denominations, many of them became disillusioned with the academic establishment in general.

This disillusionment occurred in a series of subtle shifts. The fundamentalists were worried about the growing influence of evolutionary thought. And their worries were legitimate, insofar as evolution was often linked to a thoroughly naturalistic worldview dedicated to replacing religious belief. But some believers found it easy to go from anti-evolution as a naturalistic "ism," to anti-science, and then more generally to anti-scholarship. At a fundamentalist "Bible camp" I attended in my early teens, we learned a poem that went like this:

> *Once I was a monkey, long and thin.*
> *Then I was a froggie with my tail tucked in.*
> *Then I was a baboon in a tropical tree.*
> *And now I am a professor with a Ph.D.*

Not that the fundamentalists gave up on education as such. But many of them placed their bets on "Bible institutes" with a focus on "practical training" in evangelism, missions, and church leadership. One of those institutes even had as its motto, "Our only textbook, the Bible."

SEVEN

Humility and Hope

I N THE AFTERMATH OF the horrible events of September 11, 2001, some op-ed writers in the popular media argued that the destruction in New York City had finally exposed the superficiality of the views attributed to the "postmodernists." They mentioned in particular the work of Stanley Fish, a scholar well known for his "postmodern" proclivities.

Professor Fish was not happy about this. He was particularly exercised by the charge that he and others had been teaching that it is impossible to say whether one person's views on important matters are "truer" than another's. In other words, the charge that he was an absolute relativist. So, in *Harper's Magazine,* he wrote a response to his critics.

He began his defense by asserting that he does indeed believe in objective truth. "The problem is not that there is no universal," he says; "the universal, the absolutely true, exists, and I know what it is. The problem is that you know it, too, and that we know different things." This leaves us in a predicament where we are both "armed with universal judgments that are irreconcilable, all dressed up with nowhere to go for an authoritative adjudication." We are "finite situated human beings," Fish reminds his readers, and this means that

> [w]e have to live with the knowledge of two things: that we are absolutely right and that there is no generally accepted measure by which our rightness can be independently validated. That's just the way it is, and we should just get on with it, acting in accordance with our true beliefs (what else could we do!) without expecting that some God will descend, like the duck in the old Groucho Marx TV show, and tell us that we have uttered the true and secret word.[7]

Christians who struggle with these same issues will want to think very seriously about the implications of what for Professor Fish seems to function as a throw-away line: his light-hearted reference to God. We believe that there really is a God and that this God does have access to all that is necessary to decide between competing interpretations of reality. But we human beings are not God. That is surely a very fundamental Christian conviction — one that lies at the heart of the biblical warnings against idolatry. This means that we share an important element of Fish's assessment of the human condition: we are, all of us, finite situated human beings.

Where we differ from Fish, of course, is in our equally strong conviction that the Lord of heaven and earth is neither finite nor situated. And this is what allows us to — using Fish's own phrase — "just get on with it." We too can act in the light of what we are firmly convinced to be our true beliefs about the nature of reality — always recognizing that we presently "see in a mirror, dimly," but that someday we will "see face to face" (1 Corinthians 13:12).

It is precisely because we are finite beings — and if that were not bad enough, fallen ones as well — that we must take a humbly modest approach to human knowing. God alone knows all things. We humans are mere creatures of God, limited, both individually and collectively, to our finite places in the larger scheme of things. The challenge, then, is to keep reminding ourselves that at the heart of the Christian message is the insistence that we are all finite sinners, limited yet regularly tempted to arrogance and self-centeredness.

EIGHT

Navigating the "Square Inches"

A BIG CHANGE BEGAN to occur in evangelicalism during the years immediately following World War II. One of the key motivating factors in the forming of the "neo-evangelical" movement was the desire for a renewed evangelical intellectual engagement. There were calls for a "new apologetics," and books were written that envisioned a "remaking of the Western mind."

We Christians, it was argued, have our own presuppositions in our engagement with intellectual challenges. So our task is to demonstrate to the larger world that a scholarship flowing from a genuinely Christian worldview is a plausible — even superior — alternative to other systems of thought.

This turn of events was certainly a positive thing. Many of us who engage in Christian scholarship today are deeply indebted to those neo-evangelicals who earned the scorn of their fundamentalist peers for insisting on the importance of the life of the mind.

The problem, though, was that the call to scholarly engagement sometimes took on a triumphalist tone, moving from separation to an attempt at domination.

I experienced a bit of this in my own attitudes in my younger days. In my own quest for an appropriate model for doing Christian scholarship, I was greatly influenced early on — and still am — by the example of the 19th-century Dutch scholar and statesman Abraham Kuyper. On the occasion of the founding of the Free University (Vrije Universiteit) of Amsterdam, Kuyper gave an inaugural address in which he issued his oft-quoted (including by me) manifesto that "there is not a square inch in the whole domain of our human existence over which Christ, who is sovereign over all, does not cry: 'Mine!'"[8]

I continue to find that inspiring. But I also see the danger of employing it in triumphalist terms, implying that we need to go "out there" in the broader academy and conquer all of those square inches in the name of Christ. I much prefer to link Kuyper's manifesto to an important word of counsel from the evangelical philosopher Arthur Holmes. Christians, he said, need to live in the tension between "epistemic humility" and "epistemic hope."[9] We confess that only the Creator has a clear and comprehensive knowledge of all things. This should inspire in us a deep humility. But we also have received the promise that God will eventually, in the end-time, lead us into that mode of perfect knowing that is proper to us as human creatures.

In all of this we can operate with a significant measure of hope. We can endure what Frank Gaebelein described as "the discipline of self-restraint and plain hard work" without giving in to despair or cynicism.

NINE

A Communal Task

A CADEMIC ACTIVITIES ARE NOT performed by iso-
lated individuals — they are functions of academic
community. The great universities founded on European
and North American soil were established and sustained
over the centuries by communities of people who be-
lieved that the academic calling had a profound religious
significance.

As Lutheran scholar Mark Schwehn has pointed out in his
important book *Exiles from Eden: Religion and the Academic
Vocation,* these intellectual communities were undergirded
by such "spiritual" virtues as humility, faith, self-denial, and
love. These qualities, Schwehn observes, were sustained in
past academic settings by affections, liturgical practices, and
symbol systems that were intimately intertwined with religious convictions; and, as Schwehn boldly states his case,
"their continued vitality would seem to be in some jeopardy
under wholly secular auspices." Indeed, Schwehn strongly
suspects that "most of our present-day academies" are "living
off a kind of borrowed fund of moral capital."[10]

The virtues featured in Schwehn's account are not a mere pious gloss for academic life. They provide the cement that gives cohesiveness to the academic enterprise. Humility translates in very concrete ways into a spirit of critical self-examination necessary for a healthy intellectual quest. Faith builds the trust and reliance on others that is foundational to a community of scholars. Self-denial and love of other people — along with love of one's subject matter — reinforce the patterns of scholarly teaching and dialogue. And honesty is an absolute scholarly necessity, both in reporting what we have discovered and in treating the work of other scholars.

Neither does Schwehn shrink from pointing out that in the past these spiritual virtues were themselves grounded in practices of communal worship in the academic setting. It is unreasonable, of course, to expect that such practices can be reintroduced into the present-day academy on a wide-scale basis. It is not unreasonable, however, to contemplate that some groups of scholars — those who have not abandoned the religious convictions that were once widely accepted in the academy — could bear witness in their own scholarly lives to the connections among academic tasks, spiritual virtues, and communal worship. This is one of the key strategies that Schwehn proposes: those religious academic institutions in which worship and the spiritual disciplines can still be openly encouraged must keep the connections alive, resisting the secularizing forces that have already caused widespread academic disintegration.

This talk about academic "disintegration" can, of course, be seen as an echo of the somewhat more apocalyptic scenario sketched in the concluding paragraph of philosopher Alasdair MacIntyre's *After Virtue*. There MacIntyre called for "the construction of local forms of community within which civility and the intellectual and moral life can be sustained through the new dark ages which are already upon us." This time around, MacIntyre insists, "the barbarians are not waiting beyond the frontiers; they have already been governing us for quite some time." Our only hope is to wait "for another — doubtless very different — St. Benedict."[11]

Apocalyptic scenarios have a certain attractiveness for evangelicals, and it is tempting to link the call for intellectual integrity to MacIntyre's "Benedictine" option: since the rest of the academy has lost its moorings, why don't we withdraw into strong, faith-based academic communities where we maintain the patterns of civility in our internal communal lives?

But such an alternative is defective, mainly because it fails to recognize the historic intent of the actual "Benedictine" option. The monastic tradition in Roman Catholicism was never seen simply as an abandonment of everything that existed beyond the boundaries of the abbey. Monastic communities existed to keep certain communally based virtues alive in a way that would strengthen the larger church, and even the larger human community. Monastic communities formed a subset of a broader system of "orders," all of which were seen as making a contribution to the overall social and cultural scheme of things.

Religiously based academic institutions certainly have an important role to play in this regard. As noted earlier, Mark Schwehn makes a forceful case for their existence in the present-day confusions of academic life. But Schwehn also rightly observes that not all of us can — or should — work in Christian institutions. Sustaining networks of Christian scholars who work in other, more secular academic settings is also crucial — especially when good patterns of communication and mutual edification are established among those scholars who are pursuing their vocations in diverse contexts.

So, then, it is helpful to think of the formation of religious "orders" in the academy. Christians scholars in general can function like, say, Jesuits or Franciscans, who may live and work together in the same institution or bond with scholars in other institutions in a commitment to a shared vocation.

Just before I finished my studies at the University of Chicago to join the faculty at Calvin College, I received a letter from a veteran professor at Calvin, an accomplished scholar in "Middle English" literature. Welcoming me to the Calvin faculty, he noted that I was making an important commitment in this assignment. "Many of us can be at other places, at excellent secular schools," he said. "But we are at Calvin because we have taken special vows — it is sort of like becoming a monk" — but "without the celibacy!" He went on: "To teach at this school is to respond to a special calling — to take this community, this theological tradition, with utmost seriousness, and working to make it a healthy tradition by a shared commitment to creative teaching and scholarship."

That was immensely important counsel for me. It still influences the way I see the Christian scholarly community. Our shared "vows," again, are not for all of us to be in the same place doing exactly the same kind of service. We are a diaspora, a vow-based community "in dispersion." But it is important to take those shared vows seriously, in order — as my late colleague put it — to nurture "a healthy tradition by a shared commitment to creative teaching and scholarship."

TEN

Mutual Encouragement

A CAMPUS MINISTRY AT a state university invited me
to speak to a gathering of Christian students. Shortly
after accepting the assignment, I was contacted by the chair
of the Philosophy Department at the university. A student
had told him about my forthcoming visit and asked if I
would also be willing to give a more scholarly technical
paper to faculty and graduate students on how I saw Christian faith as influencing the substance of political thought.
I was honored by the invitation and agreed to do it.

The Philosophy Department arranged for two scholars
to respond to my paper, one a philosopher and the other a
political scientist. I was told ahead of time that neither of
them was known to be a religious believer.

The philosopher's response to my presentation was pre-
dictably provocative, and then the political scientist took
the podium. This is how he began: "I have taught at this
university for about two decades, and today I want to say
something that I have never said in a public setting here
before. I am a Christian — I consider myself to be a com-

mitted Catholic believer. And I want to tell you why I am making that declaration at the beginning of this response to Professor Mouw's paper."

He then reported that the previous year, on the printed program of the annual convention of the American Political Science Association (which he regularly attended), he saw that a group of Christians had scheduled a session focusing on the role of faith in the study of political science. Out of curiosity he went to the session. He was surprised that it was a good-sized audience as those sessions go, and most of the political scientists present were either evangelicals or Catholics.

He said he was profoundly moved by the phenomenon of scholars willing openly to wrestle with the connection between their faith and their scholarly subject matter. When they passed a sheet of paper around for people to express an interest in being a part of the group, he decided to sign up. "I need to tell all of you about that," he went on, "so that you will understand why I am going to express my basic agreement — with a few minor points of difference — with the paper Mouw has just read."

After the session — which was a lively one — I thanked him for his personal words. He told me that he was a bit nervous about saying what he had said but that meeting with the group at the convention had given him the courage to, as he put it, "come out of the closet as a believer."

This political scientist had for several decades been a faithful Christian and a serious scholar. But that day he announced that he had recently become a member of a "religious order."

ELEVEN

Safe Spaces for "Playing Around"

O NE DAY A PHILOSOPHY colleague at Calvin College told me about a conversation he had just had with a student who visited his office. The student informed the professor that he had become an atheist. "What year are you in?" my colleague asked. "I'm a junior," came the reply. "Oh," said my colleague. "You are a year behind where I was as a college student. I went through my atheist year as a sophomore!"

That may have been a bit condescending on my colleague's part. But the story points to something helpful in thinking about Christian higher education. It is good to promote a "safe-space" atmosphere for serious intellectual engagement.

I like the idea of "safe spaces" for dealing with tough issues. Over a decade ago a Mormon scholar and I agreed to codirect a dialogue between a small group of Mormons and an equal number of evangelicals, focusing on our theological differences. Since the convening institutions would be Fuller Seminary, along with Brigham Young University, and I knew that this could be somewhat controversial in the evangelical world, I invited my Mormon counterpart to meet with our Board of Trustees to offer his perspective on the project. He won our trustees over with his candor. "We Mormons have not had serious contact with historic Christianity for at least a century-and-a-half. We're not even sure we are using the right theological vocabulary in explaining our views on key topics. Fuller is offering us a safe space to try out our formulations. We need that!"

Safe spaces are crucial for intellectual explorations. If a bright student is going to decide to be an atheist or an agnostic, I would hope that this would happen in a Christian setting where his or her questions are taken seriously. My own most challenging period of religious doubt took place during graduate studies on secular campuses. Spiritually it was a very lonely time. I'm grateful for the "love that would not let me go" through those difficult times. But I still wish it had happened during earlier years when I was in a "safer" environment for facing those challenges.

If we are going to make the case for safe spaces in Christian higher education, we need to find them in our own personal scholarly lives. I had a colleague, a well-known scholar, who would often end hallway conversations by saying, "Well, I have to get back to my office and play around with a few ideas." Intellectual engagement as "playing around." To be sure, scholarship is a serious business. But it is precisely because it is so serious that we need to relax a bit in our scholarly engagements. It's something like getting your blood pressure checked. The need to have it checked can be a serious business. But the test will be accurate only if you can stop concentrating on how serious it is. The instrument used will reveal the truth only if you are able to relax.

Good spiritual resources are available to help us lighten up a little in our scholarly pursuits, and it is important to demonstrate the power of these resources to our students. The most important of these resources, I am convinced, is something I have already been emphasizing in these pages: the cultivation of the combination of "epistemic humility" and "epistemic hope." God is God and we are not. What a relief! And what a marvelous basis for relaxing a bit and approaching the big challenges of scholarship and teaching with a good dose of genuinely pious playfulness!

TWELVE

Academic "Body Life"

THERE IS A DIVERSITY of gifts in the Christian community. Christians are members of a Body, and bodies
have various limbs and organs. Not every part contributes
to the well-being of the life of the whole in the same way.

I hear sermons about that notion of Body, especially as
it applies to congregations. In the congregation are many
functions, many gifts. Some sing in the choir; others make
the coffee; and there are deacons, elders, pastors, commit-
tee members, Sunday school teachers, and custodians.

But the message about diverse gifts is true of other areas of service as well. That it holds for academic communities is something I had to learn in several stages. To be
sure, I was aware of it in one sense from the beginning.
Early on in graduate school, for example, I learned that
the departmental secretary had an influence that went far
beyond her pay grade!

A new level of awareness happened, however, when our
son started college on the campus where I had been teaching for fifteen years. Suddenly I became aware of realities

about which I had been only vaguely aware for a decade and a half — dormitories, resident directors, and academic advisors now became a part of my consciousness.

I entered into yet another stage of awareness when I became a senior administrator. I found out what admissions officers actually do, as well as fund-raisers, the folks in the payroll department, office managers, trustees. In the academic institution, as in the congregation, many functions, many gifts.

But there is also diversity among scholars as such. As a visiting lecturer on a university campus, I had a conversation with a faculty member about one of his colleagues. "A good guy," the faculty member said, "but he is a mere popularizer of the high-level scholarship the rest of us produce."

I wondered about the word "mere" in this case. The scholar with whom I was speaking was in a field of expertise different than mine, but one I feel I should know something about. I found this person's writings a bit difficult to stay with. But I had read a well-written book by his "popularizer" colleague, and I had found it extremely helpful. The book did not have a lot of footnotes, but there were several references to the work of the scholar with whom I was now speaking.

I am an avid consumer of technical scholarship in the areas that matter most to me. But I am also grateful for "mere popularizers" who enlighten me about other fields of intellectual inquiry. They have an important role in the broader scholarly community. And the same holds for those who spend more time than others in mentoring students and writing extensive critical comments in response to answers to exam questions and term papers. And also (not to be too self-serving!) for those who have chosen to expend much energy in academic administration.

THIRTEEN

Academic "Hopes and Fears"

A UNIVERSITY-SPONSORED CONFERENCE I attended on "the academic vocation" urged the speakers to talk in very personal terms about their own scholarly pilgrimages. I was impressed by the candor of the presentations. Scholars who clearly could be termed successful talked about the experiences of vulnerability that had plagued them along the way: the fear of failure, worries about peer disapproval, tensions with colleagues.

"The hopes and fears of all the years." We sing about them in the familiar Advent carol, and they are a real presence in the years of a scholar's life as well. Our hopes get us started on our scholarly journeys, and they motivate us at crucial points along the way. But at every stage in the journey there are also fears. In my case, I have sometimes been fearful about continuing to travel on well-trod paths. At other times, I have been fearful of taking new paths.

I often find Simone Weil provocative in an inspiring way. Here is one of her most provocative comments: "Christ likes us to prefer truth to him," she says, "because, before being Christ, he is truth. If one turns aside from him to go toward the truth, one will not go far before falling into his arms."[12]

I have thought much about this comment. For one thing, it reminds me reassuringly of the words of the well-known hymn John Henry Newman wrote as he was leaving an influential position in the Anglican Church to step out into what was for him the uncharted territory of Roman Catholicism:

Lead, kindly Light, amid th' encircling gloom,
Lead Thou me on!
The night is dark, and I am far from home;
Lead Thou me on!
Keep Thou my feet; I do not ask to see
The distant scene; one step enough for me.

Simone Weil and John Henry Newman are both de-scribing the experience of stepping out in faith into the un-known. For Simone Weil it is taking steps into uncharted territory, knowing — in spite of one's fears — that there are arms out there somewhere that are ready to embrace you. For Newman it is the sense of being led into the darkness by a light source that promises to continue to illuminate the way, step by step, no matter how dark the path before you may presently appear.

These images speak to very real experiences I have had in my own academic journey. When, for example, after two decades of fulltime teaching and scholarship — a way of academic life that I had never thought of giving up for anything else — I agreed to move into a senior position in academic administration, I did so in very much of a Weil-Newman state of heart and mind. I hoped that Jesus was out there somewhere to catch me, and I prayed for a light to illumine what looked for all the world like a dark pathway.

But I have also thought much about how the stepping-into-the-unknown imagery captures something important to intellectual inquiry in particular. The scholarly life is an ongoing series of steps into the unknown. Every time we pick up a new book to read, or choose a new topic to write about for an essay assignment, or map out a new research project, or agree to take or teach a new course, we are taking some steps into uncharted territory. In our intellectual pursuits we are regularly stepping out on new adventures.

Not that the normal routines of the academic life require highly dramatic imagery. Most of the new ventures on which we set forth do not occur "amid th' encircling gloom." The light and darkness motifs are best reserved for the "big" moments of stepping out in faith. But for the Christian scholar, it is always appropriate to invoke the support of the everlasting arms.

To acknowledge the "hopes and fears" of the scholarly pilgrimage is to acknowledge, among other things, the frequent encounter with loneliness. Indeed, when we are focusing on scholarship as such, loneliness is more often than not the name of the game.

Community is the context of our scholarship. It is what gives us encouragement. It provides necessary services: services from people who work in libraries; from folks who help us with the technology that is so important to our labors; from the men and women who find the funds to support our efforts; from the students whose tuition makes much of what goes on in academic communities possible — and from many others, including, of course, our colleagues, fellow travelers in academe who offer encouragement and critique.

But there are also those times when we will inevitably suffer alone — and in ways difficult to explain, even to family members and close friends outside the academy.

To be sure, most folks, academics or non-academics, can understand what it is like to be troubled by tensions in the workplace, by job insecurity, by assignments that seem impossible to fulfill. But there are also those lonely moments that only a serious scholar can understand: spending hours trying to solve an intellectual puzzle or to find the right sentence to start off a chapter. Worrying about how to be kind in reviewing a book that you think is pretty bad. Losing two days of complicated work when your computer crashes. Lying awake at night thinking about what a student said in an evaluation of your teaching.

Our communal involvement with other Christian scholars is important. And one way that it is important is that it provides us with the spiritual resources to face the inevitable times of loneliness. Indeed, it is a shame that churches don't seem eager to develop those resources for those of us who often experience the loneliness of the long-distance scholar. We might even pray, then, that the Christian community at large will begin to provide us with those necessary spiritual support systems. But those support systems will not be able to eliminate entirely the loneliness that is so much the stuff of the scholarly life.

FOURTEEN

Critique as a "Moment"

WHEN MY CHRISTIAN COLLEGE teachers described for us undergraduates the goals of Christian liberal arts education, they often quoted a line from the great 19th-century British writer Matthew Arnold, who had written about the need "to see life steadily and see it whole." I can't recall coming across this line anywhere in recent years, though. Part of the reason may be that Arnold himself seems to have fallen out of fashion — the experts no longer point as much to his writings as a model of excellence in literature. But the actual conviction expressed in that one line is also not very popular these days. When most of our contemporaries in the academy talk these days in lofty terms about higher education — when they rise above, for example, descriptions of the marketability of a specific course of study — they are more likely to wax eloquent about the benefits of "critical thinking."

My early academic training as a philosopher took place in an intellectual environment where critical thinking was taken to be pretty much the be-all and end-all of philosophical reflection. And this served me well on the path to intellectual maturity. As someone trained in that tradition of analytic critique, however, I must confess that I have regularly had to fight a new temptation: to linger over the questions as if that lingering were itself the primary goal of the life of the mind — and to encourage my students and colleagues to do the same.

I once heard the sociologist Peter Berger remark that he found most of his secular colleagues taking it for granted that "ecstasy" — in the sense of *ex stasis*, standing apart from, intellectual detachment — was the most prized moment in the intellectual quest. I must admit that I struggle against that tendency within myself.

We need to see critical thinking as one way in which we serve the Lord. Christian teaching and scholarship should aim at the ultimate goal of getting clearer in our hearts and minds about the basic issues of life in order more effectively to promote the cause of God's Kingdom. And that means asking probing questions about our shared assumptions and perspectives.

In trying to get clear about the legitimate role of the *ex-stasis* posture, I have been helped by a pair of images that philosopher C. Stephen Evans employed back in the 1970s, in a fine little book on the topic of despair. In exploring the relevance to Christian thought of the existentialist celebration of despair that was so popular at the time, he distinguished between despair as a "moment" and despair "a way of life."[13]

That same distinction applies nicely, I think, to critical

distancing. *Ex stasis* needs to happen, but as a necessary moment in the rhythms of our intellectual lives, and not as a sustained way of life.

The 19th-century Dutch theologian Herman Bavinck is reported to have said somewhere that the Christian must undergo two conversions: one conversion away from the world and another conversion back to the world.

The intellectual life should also be shaped by two similar "conversions." It is a good thing to be converted away from an exclusive focus on what we normally take for granted. But, having taking an honest look at such things, we need then to "re-convert" that lived world. By stepping back from reality in order to contemplate that reality in new ways, we can learn to love it more deeply and serve it more faithfully.

FIFTEEN

Reality Lovers

MY SON TOLD ME about a woman in the university town where he was studying who distributed a business card listing the services she offered to the community. Along with announcing such specialties as herbal healing, therapeutic massage, and the like, she described herself as an "ontological coach." I don't know how she would have further spelled out that item in her job description, but it does strike me that Christian scholarship will inevitably include an ontological coaching function. In addition to our specific areas of expertise, we all need to maintain a second specialty in the study of being-in-general, in the nature of deep reality as such.

Craig Dykstra, for many years the person at the Lilly Foundation in charge of funding religious programs and projects, got at this aspect of our academic calling when he told a group of Christian liberal arts faculty members that their teaching should focus on shaping persons "who see deeply into the reality of things and who love that reality — over time and across circumstances."[14] Similarly, the philosopher Albert Borgmann also urges Christian scholars, in a time when so much scholarship limits itself, he says, to the *surfaces* of reality, to rediscover "the eloquence of things" in their particularity, so as to find "the depth of the world."[15]

We serve a God who cares about the depths — and the breadth and the heights — of the reality that he has created: "The earth is the LORD's and the fullness thereof, the world and all who dwell therein" (Psalm 24:1). We scholars study various aspects of that world, but we must do it in the awareness that what we focus on is indeed a part of the fullness of a created reality that we are also called to love — and in loving to *see*, so that we can make connections and cultivate a proper awe and sense of mystery about the depths of created being.

The world desperately needs lovers of created reality, people who look deeply into the fullness, and especially, but of course not exclusively, into the complex created fullness that is displayed in human beings — the psalmist's "all who dwell therein" — in all of their marvelous diversity. To love reality in its depths means that we cannot help but grieve over the brokenness and woundedness of God's world in its present condition. And we know that to do so is to share in the sorrows that reside in the deep places of God's own being.

SIXTEEN

Honoring Creation

I STOPPED BELIEVING IN a "young earth" when I was a high school student. And it wasn't because of the influence of any "godless" biology teacher. The one who convinced me was a solidly evangelical scholar: I read Bernard Ramm's 1954 book *A Christian View of Science and the Scriptures*. I was motivated to read the book partly because so many in my fundamentalist world were criticizing it. For a Christian teenager in those environs to read Ramm's book was like sneaking off with a copy of *Playboy*! But I learned much from what he had to say about faith and science, and his basic approach has stayed with me over the years.

I got to know Bernie Ramm in his later years, and I asked him about the controversy in the 1950s over his views. He smiled and said that he had been willing to put up with the harassment because he had written out of a spiritual concern for the bright evangelical students he knew at the time. He did not want them going off to places like Harvard convinced that to be an evangelical is to give literalist answers to questions about the age of the earth and a universal flood — only to then experience a crisis of faith that alienated them from their evangelical roots. I thanked him for his courage.

I don't mean to dwell here on debates over evolution and the like. But I do need to say that I regret the way that the "creationist" label has come to be identified almost exclusively with a certain way of interpreting the relevance of Genesis 1 to theories about fossils and such.

Creation has a much larger significance. Believing in a created order means something important for the very way in which we view our scholarly explorations. In an intellectual climate in which there is so much emphasis on "constructing" truths, we Christians have to insist that truth is to be discovered and not created by us.

This is a wonderful comfort for those of us who take on the intellectual quest as truth-seekers. There really is something out there to look for! Our ability to grasp the ordering patterns of God's creative activity may be seriously impaired by our sinfulness. And even where sin does not prohibit us, our finitude always comes into play. For all of that, though, "the earth is the LORD's" (Psalm 24:1), and we are invited to celebrate it by deeply exploring it. To confess that is to truly be a creationist!

SEVENTEEN

Beholders

THE FIRST PHILOSOPHY COURSE I ever taught was in a university department where textbooks were prescribed by the department for all introductory courses. I had to begin the course lecturing on materials in a book of readings from the pre-Socratic philosophers. Actually, "readings" is a bit of an exaggeration. Most of what we have from those early Greek thinkers are mere fragments. And even when we have a little more to work with, it isn't always easy to figure out what they might have been getting at in some of their mysterious sayings — although we get a little help from later commentators like Aristotle, who seemed to have some idea of the basic thrust of what some of them were thinking.

I did manage to come up with a whole one-hour class lecture on the thought of Thales of Miletos (624-546 BC). He is generally considered to be the first philosopher, and he is best known for his statement, reported later by Aristotle, that everything is ultimately composed of water. It was actually an enjoyable challenge to get students thinking about the fact that, while his answer may not be all that interesting, his asking of the question about the basic "stuff" of reality was a creative initiative that got an important conversation going in Western thought.

I had a more difficult time, however, doing much with thinkers like Anaxagoras of Klazomenai. All I had available from the textbook were some fragments, preserved by a much later philosopher named Simplicius of Cilicia. And many of the fragments are rather enigmatic sayings.

I was surprised, then, to come across more recently an interesting quotation from Anaxagoras in a delightful little book by Josef Pieper, a Catholic philosopher who produced some significant works in the past century. *Only the Lover Sings* is a slight volume of talks Pieper gave to a group gathered in the studio of a sculptor friend. In one of those talks Pieper reports that Anaxagoras, while engaging in a catechetical exercise, answered the question, "Why are you here on earth?" with the stark reply, "To behold."[16] I don't know where Pieper found that quotation. If it had been one of the fragments that I had in my textbook, I might have been able to milk another lecture on Anaxagoras from that simple remark!

Pieper applied Anaxagoras's comment to the artistic task, but it holds as well for Christian scholarship. God has placed us on this earth "to behold." Beholding is that special kind of "seeing" that, as Pieper puts it, is directed to more than "the tangible surface of reality." This kind of seeing, Pieper further observes, must be "guided by love" — as the ancient mystics put it, *ubi amor, ibi oculus* (roughly, "where there is love, there is seeing").

All that we encounter in our scholarship is a part of the fullness of a created reality that we are also called to love — and in loving to see, to behold, so that we can make connections and cultivate a proper awe and sense of mystery in the presence of the depths of created being.

EIGHTEEN

Being Like Jesus in the Academy

THIS VERSE FROM AN old Gospel hymn sometimes goes through my mind.

Be like Jesus, this my song,
in the home and in the throng.
Be like Jesus all day long,
I would be like Jesus.

What does that say about how we follow Jesus in the academic "throng"? In classrooms, departmental meetings, seminars, ceremonial convocations, major academic conventions?

I have to confess that "being like Jesus" has not been an important theme for me. I never wore one of those "WWJD" bracelets. "What would Jesus do?" is not something that I think to ask when faced with a difficult decision. As an ethicist, I am much more inclined, when talking about where to look for ethical guidance, to recommend that people climb Mount Sinai, rather than the Mount on which Jesus taught.

In my theology I tend not to focus on what Jesus did that we could not possibly do. We are lost sinners who can not get ourselves out of the mess created by our shared re-bellion. Jesus came to do for us what we could not possibly do for ourselves — going to Calvary on our behalf. Rather than "the imitation of Christ," I have thought more about the ways in which he is "inimitable."

And, to be sure, there is much that we should not try to imitate, even in the years of Jesus' earthly ministry before the final week. Suppose we plan a large gathering, to last more than a day, but we forget to order the food. What would Jesus do? Or suppose we are stuck on an island and find it necessary to get back to the mainland, but we have no boat. What would Jesus do?

More seriously, it is difficult to think about what Jesus would do in facing the big challenges of contemporary life. Dilemmas in bioethics. Alternatives to Social Security. The details of immigration reform. Countering a terrorist threat.

Not that there is no way of thinking Christianly about such matters. To do so is at the heart of the Christian life. But "What would Jesus do?" is not — by itself — always a very helpful question.

For all of that, though, I know I need to pay at least some attention to the *imitatio Christi* motif. John Howard Yoder sent me back to the drawing board on this subject. He was fully aware of the inadequacies of an unnuanced "What would Jesus do?" ethic. But he still insisted that we do need to look to the example of Jesus for guidance in facing the complexities of contemporary life.

I have had some arguments with Yoder about how much we can rely on things like general revelation and a common moral consciousness — he was less optimistic about these sources than I am. But he was certainly right about this: even if there is other moral guidance available to us, we are too sinful to trust completely our ability to understand those things. What we do have, and what we can trust, is the moral example of Jesus of Nazareth. To be his disciple is to cultivate — by immersing ourselves in the practices of Christian community — the virtues that he displayed in his earthly ministry.

This is not, in Yoder's view, an unqualified imitation of Christ. "Only at one point," he wrote, "only on one subject — but then consistently and universally — is Jesus our example: in his cross." We are called to Christ-like suffering.

What might that mean for our lives in the academy, in the "throngs" that we navigate as scholars who teach, write, and engage in collegial activities with peers? How can we, in that context, as followers of Jesus, manifest the virtues that he displayed in his earthly ministry?

We come back to Mark Schwehn's observation that intellectual communities can be sustained in the long run only by the cultivation of such "spiritual" virtues as humility, faith, self-denial, and love. What does it mean to carry our crosses in the academy?

During my scholarly career I have devoted a lot of my own attention to examining various understandings of Christian involvement in public life. Not surprisingly, I have quite consistently made a point of praising the Calvinist understanding of such matters. But in recent years, while not forsaking my Calvinist convictions, I have felt compelled to acknowledge the need for a modest Lutheran corrective to any thoroughgoing Calvinism. The need for doing this was impressed upon me when I agreed to write a review of Harro Hopfl's anthology, published in the Cambridge series of "Texts in the History of Political Thought," of the writings of Luther and Calvin. As I directly compared the political writings of the two Reformers, I was struck by the irony that Calvin, who is well known for his emphasis on the ravages of sin in human affairs, showed a surprising lack of sensitivity to the tragic dimensions of politics. Here Luther actually seemed to be the better Calvinist. In his wonderful essay "On Secular Authority," Luther warns that the Christian prince must be ever vigilant if he wants his public service to be pleasing to the Lord. And even when the prince does all that he can to promote the cause of righteousness, Luther quickly adds, he should fully expect that he "will soon feel the cross lying on his neck."

Luther's counsel applies also to our work as Christian scholars. We cannot avoid the weight of the cross as we attempt to fulfill our callings. For some of us the cross's pressure on our necks will mean that we have to keep at our "ordinary" research and teaching projects even as our television screens and news websites replay, over and over again, horrible scenes of human suffering. For others it will mean that we must fight the temptation to pursue the ordinary, as we revise our scholarly plans in order to address more directly the ongoing crises. This is why we need Christian scholarly networks, communities where the spiritual gifts are nurtured, so that we can assist each other as we seek to discern the promptings of the Spirit for our individual and collective scholarly pursuits.

Pastor Tim Keller has told a wonderful story about a woman he met when he was greeting worshippers after a Sunday morning service at New York's Redeemer Presbyterian Church. She told him she had started attending services even though she was not a Christian — and she hoped she could meet with him to talk to him about matters of faith.

Tim asked her what brought her to church, and she told him about a work situation in which she had made a serious mistake in one of her assignments. When the CEO called her to account for her error, her immediate manager intervened and told the CEO that he was the one who was really responsible for the mistake.

Afterward, she expressed her gratitude — and surprise — to her manager. She had often had people take credit for good things she had done, she told him, but never before had someone taken the blame for a mistake she had made. He responded that he felt obliged to do so, because as a Christian he knew Christ to be his Savior: Christ had taken the blame for him. She wanted to know more about this kind of faith!

That is a fine example of the kind of self-sacrificing collegiality we can bring with us as we follow Jesus in the academy. And undergirding that is a Christlike humility.

NINETEEN

A Loom for Weaving

I N A SONNET COMPOSED in 1939, Edna St. Vincent Millay wrote some lines that many see as a kind of secular prophecy being fulfilled in our day:

> *Upon this age, that never speaks its mind,*
> *This furtive age, this age endowed with power*
> *To wake the moon with footsteps, fit an oar*
> *Into the rowlocks of the wind, and find*
> *What swims before his prow, what swirls behind —*
> *Upon this gifted age, in its dark hour,*
> *Rains from the sky a meteoric shower*
> *Of facts . . . they lie unquestioned, uncombined.*
> *Wisdom enough to leech us of our ill*
> *Is daily spun; but there exists no loom*
> *To weave it into fabric. . . .*[17]

The imagery here does seem to speak to much of what characterizes higher education these days: the proliferation of knowledge — facts and findings that seem to come down upon us as a "meteoric" downpour; Google searches that produce thousands of results that simply appear on our screens, "unquestioned, uncombined," as we scroll.

Indeed, many of our contemporaries celebrate the absence of any "loom" that can combine the fragments of our intellectual lives into a coherent whole. The rejection of the "tyranny of the metanarrative" is for such people one of the triumphs of postmodern existence.

We have no easy Christian response to this advocacy of fragmentation. The best we can come up with is the combination of "epistemic humility" and "epistemic hope": "Now I know only in part; then I will know fully, even as I have been fully known" (1 Corinthians 13:12).

We can also take our cue here from a passage that occurs about mid-point in Plato's *Meno*. Socrates' friends are discouraged at that stage in the discussion, because they have been looking for a unified definition of virtue — but instead, all they have come up with, under Socrates' persistent questioning, is a "swarm" of virtues. We can't go on, they tell the philosopher.

At this point, Socrates' tone shifts to the pastoral. Don't get discouraged by swarms, Socrates tells them. Appearances to the contrary, he says, "all nature is akin." This means, he assures them, that there is nothing to hinder us, having tackled just one small assignment in the epistemic quest, from going on to find out about all of the rest, as long as we do "not weary in seeking."[18]

Christian scholars can take heart from similar sentiments — but with even better grounds than Socrates had

— for not getting disillusioned in the important process of attending to the complexities of the intellectual quest. Because of the One in whom all reality coheres, we can explore that reality with a profound love for that which we are studying.

The reality we study as scholars is, to be sure, often "swarmy." But as Christians we can proceed patiently, and with an ultimate confidence that it all really does hang together. And we can do so with a sense of safety as we proceed. Simone Weil's word of encouragement again: to step out in the cause of truth is to move in the direction of the One who is the Truth.

The Christian faith provides us with important spiritual resources for the complex challenges of our scholarly endeavors. We confess that only the Creator has a clear and comprehensive knowledge of all things. This should inspire in us a strong sense of the "epistemic humility" that Arthur Holmes urged upon us as scholars. But we also have received the promise that God will eventually lead us into that mode of perfect knowing that is proper to us as human creatures. This should give us a significant measure of — Holmes again — "epistemic hope."

If we effectively appropriate these attitudes — humility and hope — we can display the kind of patience that is capable of tolerating complexities and living with seemingly unconnected particularities without giving in to despair or cynicism. To show forth this kind of approach to intellectual complexities is to perform an important ministry — a Christ-like ministry — in the present-day academy.

Jesus Christ has created all things, and "he sustains all things by his powerful word" (Hebrews 1:3). That conviction provides us with a powerful motivation for taking on the demanding tasks of Christian scholarship. For here, too, we can make our way in the confidence that we are never far removed from the everlasting arms that are always there to support us.

Endnotes

1. Frank E. Gaebelein, *The Christian, the Arts, and Truth: Regaining the Vision of Greatness,* ed. D. Bruce Lockerbie (Portland, Ore.: Multnomah Press, 1985), 154-55.

2. Thomas à Kempis, *The Imitation of Christ,* trans. Robert Dudley (Wheathampstead, Hertfordshire: Anthony Clark, 1980), 1.

3. Simone Weil, *Waiting for God,* trans. Emma Craufurd (New York: Harper and Row Publishers, 1951), 106-7.

4. John Henry Newman, *The Idea of a University* (New York: Rinehart Press, 1960), 126.

5. Newman, *The Idea,* 134-35.

6. Quoted by William Ringenberg, *The Christian College: A History of Protestant Higher Education in America* (Grand Rapids: William B. Eerdmans Publishing Co., 1984), 165.

7. Stanley Fish, "Postmodern Warfare: The Ignorance of Our Warrior Intellectuals," *Harper's Magazine* (July 2002), 37-38.

8. Abraham Kuyper, "Sphere Sovereignty," in *Abraham Kuyper: A Centennial Reader,* ed. James D. Bratt (Grand Rapids: William B. Eerdmans Publishing Co., 1998), 488.

9. Arthur F. Holmes, *Contours of a World View* (Grand Rapids: Eerdmans Publishing Co., 1983), 128.

10. Mark Schwehn, *Exiles from Eden: Religion and the Academic Vocation* (New York: Oxford University Press, 2005), 55, 51.

11. Alasdair MacIntyre, *After Virtue: A Study in Moral Theory* (Notre Dame, Ind.: University of Notre Dame Press, 1981), 245.

12. Weil, *Waiting for God*, 69.

13. C. Stephen Evans, *Despair: A Moment or a Way of Life?* (Downers Grove: InterVarsity Press, 1971).

14. Craig Dykstra, "Communities of Conviction and the Liberal Arts," *The Council of Societies for the Study of Religion Bulletin*, vol. 19, no. 3 (September 1990), 62; Dykstra makes this case in greater detail in his *Vision and Character* (New York: Paulist Press, 1981).

15. Borgmann, *Crossing the Postmodern Divide* (Chicago: University of Chicago Press, 1992), 51, 82.

16. Josef Pieper, *Only the Lover Sings: Art and Contemplation*, trans. Lothar Krauth (San Francisco: Ignatius Press, 1990), 72-74.

17. Sonnet, 1939, at http://www.cscs.umich.edu/~crshalizi/Poetry/Millay/Upon_this_age.html.

18. *Meno*, section 81D, in *Plato's Meno, With Text and Essays*, ed. Malcolm Brown (New York: The Bobbs-Merrill Company, 1971), 33.